T0014544

# PAPER CRAFTS FOR KIDS

## 25 CUT-OUT ACTIVITIES FOR KIDS AGES 4-8

### STEFANIA LUCA

ROCKRIDGE PRESS

Copyright © 2020 by Rockridge Press, Emeryville, California

No part of this publication may be reproduced, stored in a retrieval system, or transmitted in any form or by any means, electronic, mechanical, photocopying, recording, scanning, or otherwise, except as permitted under Sections 107 or 108 of the 1976 United States Copyright Act, without the prior written permission of the Publisher. Requests to the Publisher for permission should be addressed to the Permissions Department, Rockridge Press, 6005 Shellmound Street, Suite 175, Emeryville, CA 94608.

Limit of Liability/Disclaimer of Warranty: The Publisher and the author make no representations or warranties with respect to the accuracy or completeness of the contents of this work and specifically disclaim all warranties, including without limitation warranties of fitness for a particular purpose. No warranty may be created or extended by sales or promotional materials. The advice and strategies contained herein may not be suitable for every situation. This work is sold with the understanding that the Publisher is not engaged in rendering medical, legal, or other professional advice or services. If professional assistance is required, the services of a competent professional person should be sought. Neither the Publisher nor the author shall be liable for damages arising herefrom. The fact that an individual, organization, or website is referred to in this work as a citation and/or potential source of further information does not mean that the author or the Publisher endorses the information the individual, organization, or website may provide or recommendations they/it may make. Further, readers should be aware that websites listed in this work may have changed or disappeared between when this work was written and when it is read.

For general information on our other products and services or to obtain technical support, please contact our Customer Care Department within the United States at (866) 744-2665, or outside the United States at (510) 253-0500.

Rockridge Press publishes its books in a variety of electronic and print formats. Some content that appears in print may not be available in electronic books, and vice versa.

TRADEMARKS: Rockridge Press and the Rockridge Press logo are trademarks or registered trademarks of Callisto Media Inc. and/or its affiliates, in the United States and other countries, and may not be used without written permission. All other trademarks are the property of their respective owners. Rockridge Press is not associated with any product or vendor mentioned in this book.

Interior and Cover Designer: Patricia Fabricant
Art Producer: Janice Ackerman
Editor: Elizabeth Baird
Production Editor: Jenna Dutton

Illustrations & Photography: © 2020 Stefania Luca

Author Photo: © 2020 Dan Luca

ISBN: Print 978-1-64739-107-2

R0

# A NOTE TO PARENTS

**Welcome to *Paper Crafts for Kids*!**

I'm Stefania Luca, a passionate kids' craft designer and the creator of the crafting website Non-Toy Gifts (NonToyGifts.com).

In this book, you'll find 25 ready-to-cut craft templates with easy step-by-step instructions for putting them together. Complete the crafts together with your child, or let them explore their creative side on their own!

Although this book offers a great variety of crafts, it requires few supplies. Most projects call for nothing more than scissors and glue. The rest require simple household objects that you likely have on hand. A goal of this book is to minimize the number of trips to the craft store so your child can get artsy and practie scissor skills whenever they want.

While most projects focus on cutting and folding, a couple also call for kids to color template images. Arts and crafts go hand in hand, and these projects give kids the opportunity to engage their creative side in more ways than one.

## A Note About Scissor Safety

While cutting with scissors is a great way for kids to develop fine motor skills, younger kids may need some help handling them safely. You know your child best. If they're struggling, be prepared to show them how to hold scissors properly, and supervise their cutting. Safety scissors are a great option for smaller hands.

**Happy crafting!**

# LIST OF CRAFTS

# HAPPY HOUSE

**TEMPLATE ON PAGE 27**

**WHAT YOU'LL NEED:** scissors, glue

**INSTRUCTIONS:**

**1** Cut out the house pattern.

**2** Fold along the dotted lines.

**3** Glue the tab marked GLUE 1 to the back of the front house panel.

**4** Glue the tabs marked GLUE 2 to one side of the roof.

**5** Glue the tabs marked GLUE 3 to the other side of the roof.

# ACTIVITY DICE

**TEMPLATE ON PAGE 29**

- - - - - - - - - - - - - - - - - -

**WHAT YOU'LL NEED:** scissors, glue

- - - - - - - - - - - - - - - - - -

**INSTRUCTIONS:**

**1** Cut out the dice pattern.

**2** Fold along the dotted lines.

**3** Apply glue to the tabs marked GLUE 1 and glue the tabs behind the number 4 face.

**4** Apply glue to the tabs marked GLUE 2 and glue the tabs behind the number 2 face.

**5** Apply glue to the tabs marked GLUE 3 and glue the rest of the faces together into a cube.

**HOW TO PLAY** with the activity dice:

**1** Roll the dice.

**2** Do the activity on the dice side that faces upward.

**3** Repeat as many times as you like!

**4** Invite a friend to play, and take turns rolling the dice.

# ORIGAMI CAT

**TEMPLATE ON PAGE 31**

- - - - - - - - - - - - - - - - - - - - - - - -

**WHAT YOU'LL NEED:** scissors

- - - - - - - - - - - - - - - - - - - - - - - -

**INSTRUCTIONS:**

**1** Cut out the cat pattern.

**2** Fold the paper in half diagonally so that you create a triangle with the cat face in the middle.

**3** Flip the folded triangle over, with the cat facedown.

**4** Fold each corner upright along the dotted lines to make the cat's ears.

**5** Fold the top center downward along the dotted line.

# LADYBUG TIC-TAC-TOE

TEMPLATE ON PAGE 33

WHAT YOU'LL NEED: scissors

INSTRUCTIONS:

**1** Cut out the ladybug template and the different colored circles.

## HOW TO PLAY:

**1** The first player places one of their tokens on one of the nine spaces on the ladybug.

**2** The second player places one of their tokens on one of the remaining spaces.

**3** The players take turns placing their tokens, until one of them manages to place three of their tokens in a horizontal, vertical, or diagonal row and be the winner.

**VARIATION:** You can also use buttons or different coins as the tokens. Just make sure that five of the buttons or coins are the same, and the other five are different from the first five but like one another.

# BUILD YOUR OWN ROBOT

**TEMPLATE ON PAGE 35**

- - - - - - - - - - - - - - - - - - - -

**WHAT YOU'LL NEED:** scissors, colored pencils or crayons, glue

- - - - - - - - - - - - - - - - - - - -

**INSTRUCTIONS:**

**1** Color all the robot parts.

**2** Cut out all the colored robot parts.

**3** Glue the robot head to the body.

**4** Glue the robot arms to the body, one on each side of the body.

**5** Glue the robot legs at the bottom of the body, one on each side of the body, as you did with the arms.

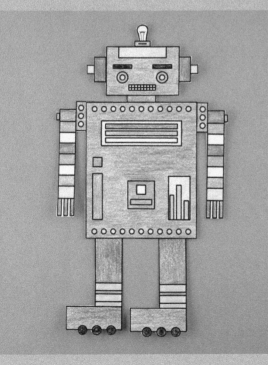

# WHIRLING WINDMILL

**TEMPLATE ON PAGE 37**

**WHAT YOU'LL NEED:** scissors, hole punch, glue, paper fastener

**INSTRUCTIONS:**

**1** Cut out the pattern pieces: (1) windmill house, (2) the four blades (circles), and (3) the blade holder (the cross).

**2** Use a hole punch to make a hole in the middle of the cross and another hole in the middle of the house roof.

**3** Fold the circles in half. The pattern side should be on the outside.

**4** Glue the folded circles onto the cross so that there is one circle on each arm of the cross. Make sure all the folded circles are facing the same direction.

**5** Insert the paper fastener first into the hole in the cross, and then the hole into the hole on house roof. Separate the two legs of the fastener and bend them over to secure the blades to the windmill house.

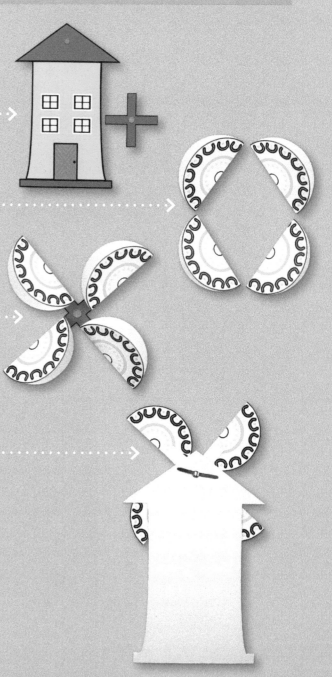

6

# OWL HAT

**TEMPLATE ON PAGE 39**

**WHAT YOU'LL NEED:**
scissors, tape or glue

**INSTRUCTIONS:**

**1** Cut out the three pieces of the owl hat.

**2** Attach one back panel to each side of the front panel of the headband using tape or glue. ········>

**3** Bring the two ends together to form a circle and attach them using tape or glue. If using glue, use just a small dot. If using tape, do not fold the top and bottom edges of the tape around the headband. This way, you can try on the headband for size and readjust it if you need to. ········>

**4** Place the hat on your head to make sure it fits.

**5** Secure the two ends together with tape or glue. If you used glue, make sure you use enough and allow it to dry. If you used tape, fold the top and bottom edges of the tape over the headband.

**VARIATION:** Older kids may use a stapler instead of tape.

# CLOTHESPIN PIRATE PUPPETS

**TEMPLATE ON PAGE 41**

- - - - - - - - - - - - - - - - - - - - - - -

**WHAT YOU'LL NEED:** scissors, glue, two wooden clothespins

- - - - - - - - - - - - - - - - - - - - - - -

**INSTRUCTIONS:**

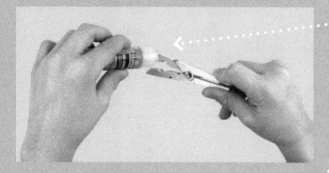

1 Cut out the two pirates.

2 Cut along the line between the upper and lower teeth.

3 Apply glue on the gripping part of the clothespins.

4 Stick the upper part of the pirates' heads onto the top part of the gripping area and the rest of the pirates' bodies onto the bottom part of the gripping area.

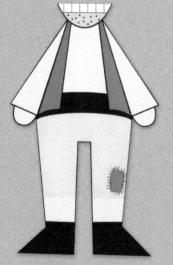

# 3D FLOWER CARD

**TEMPLATE ON PAGE 43**

**WHAT YOU'LL NEED:** scissors, glue

## INSTRUCTIONS:

**1** Cut out the yellow flower and the blue square with the flower in the middle.

**2** Write a message for someone you love on the back of the blue square.

**3** Fold the petals of the yellow flower toward the middle of the flower.

**4** Glue the middle of the flower cutout to the middle of the flower on the blue square.

# ENVELOPE SCARECROWS

**TEMPLATE ON PAGE 45**

**WHAT YOU'LL NEED:** scissors, glue, two envelopes, black marker

## INSTRUCTIONS:

**1** Cut out the hats, hair pieces, noses, and eyes for each scarecrow.

**2** Glue two matching hair pieces onto the first envelope, one on the top-right corner and the other on the top-left corner of the envelope, so that some of the "hair" sticks out. Repeat with the remaining two hair pieces and the second envelope.

**3** Glue the first hat along the top edge of one of the envelopes, on top of the hair pieces. Repeat with the second envelope.

**4** Glue the eyes under the hat on your first envelope, and then repeat with the second envelope.

**5** Glue the nose in the middle of the first envelope, under the eyes. Repeat with the second envelope.

**6** Use a black marker to draw the mouths on both scarecrows.

**TIP:** Use 6¾ size envelopes for this project.

# ORIGAMI DOG

**TEMPLATE ON PAGE 47**

---

**WHAT YOU'LL NEED:** scissors

---

**INSTRUCTIONS:**

**1** Cut out the pattern.

**2** Fold the paper in half diagonally so that you create a triangle with the dog nose at the top.

**3** Flip the paper so that the eyes are facing you, then fold the ears down along the dotted lines.

**4** Fold the bottom corner up to make the mouth.

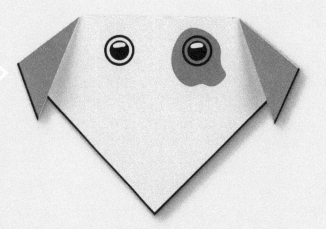

# MAKE-YOUR-OWN JIGSAW PUZZLE

**TEMPLATE ON PAGE 49**

- - - - - - - - - - - - - - - - - -

**WHAT YOU'LL NEED:** scissors

- - - - - - - - - - - - - - - - - -

**INSTRUCTIONS:**

1 Cut out the puzzle pattern.

2 Follow the lines on the back of the puzzle and cut out all the puzzle pieces.

**HOW TO SOLVE** the jigsaw puzzle:

1 Lay out your puzzle pieces on a flat surface.

2 Find the border pieces. These pieces have one or two smooth sides.

3 Put all the border pieces together to form the puzzle frame.

4 Fit the rest of the pieces together inside the puzzle frame until you see the unicorn jumping over the rainbow.

# PAPER BAG PANDA

**TEMPLATE ON PAGE 51**

**WHAT YOU'LL NEED:** black marker or crayon, paper bag, scissors, glue

**INSTRUCTIONS:**

1 Start with a black paper bag, or use a black marker or crayon to color the outside of your paper bag a solid black.

2 Cut out the panda pattern.

3 Glue the panda's head onto the bottom flap of the paper bag, lining up the bottom of the head with one of the creased sides of the flap.

4 Glue the panda's belly at the open end of the paper bag. Make sure the open end of the paper bag is facing you, or away from the head.

5 Use it as a puppet!

13

# BALANCING BUTTERFLY

**TEMPLATE ON PAGE 53**

**WHAT YOU'LL NEED:** colored pencils, scissors, tape or glue, two pennies

**INSTRUCTIONS:**

1 Color the butterfly.

2 Cut out the colored butterfly.

3 Tape or glue the pennies to the back of the butterfly's wings, one on each wing.

4 Place the butterfly on your finger and try to balance it.

# RAINBOW CLOCK

**TEMPLATE ON PAGE 55**

---

**WHAT YOU'LL NEED:** scissors, glue, paper plate, pencil, hole punch, paper fastener

---

**INSTRUCTIONS:**

**1** Cut out all 12 numbers as well as the two hands.

**2** Glue numbers 12, 3, 6, and 9 onto the paper plate.

**3** Glue the rest of the numbers onto the paper plate.

**4** Ask an adult to use a pencil to make a hole in the middle of the paper plate.

**5** Use a hole punch to make a hole at the bottom of each clock hand.

**6** Attach the hour and minute hands to the paper plate with a paper fastener.

# CURIOUS LION

## TEMPLATE ON PAGE 57

---

**WHAT YOU'LL NEED:** scissors

---

**INSTRUCTIONS:**

**1** Cut out the lion pattern.

**2** Cut the lion's mane along the dotted lines.

**3** Fold the mane strips as shown.

**VARIATION:** Use different folds for the mane strips: big folds and small folds. Leave some of the strips unfolded and see if you like how that looks, too.

# PAPER ROLL HEDGEHOG

**TEMPLATE ON PAGE 59**

**WHAT YOU'LL NEED:**
scissors, glue, paper roll

**INSTRUCTIONS:**

1 Cut out the hedgehog pattern.

2 Glue the two feet onto the hedgehog's body, one on each side of the body.

3 Glue the paper roll onto the hedgehog's prickles, making sure to align the bottom of the prickles with the bottom of the paper roll.

4 Glue the hedgehog's body to the paper roll so that both the prickles and the body are facing you.

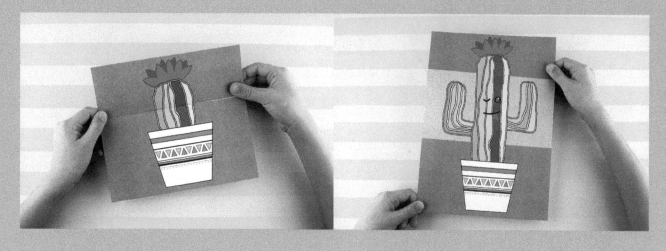

# CRAZY CACTUS SURPRISE

**TEMPLATE ON PAGE 61**

- - - - - - - - - - - - - - - - - - - - - -

**WHAT YOU'LL NEED:** scissors

- - - - - - - - - - - - - - - - - - - - - -

**INSTRUCTIONS:**

1 Cut out the gray rectangle with the cactus in the middle.

2 Place the paper facing down so the blank side is facing you.

3 Fold the paper along line 1.

4 Flip the paper over with the cactus faceup.

5 Fold the paper, with line 1 aligned on top of line 2. The light gray area will be tucked inside.

6 Open and close the folded part to see the crazy cactus appear and disappear!

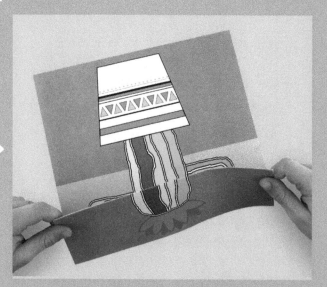

# ANIMAL FINGER PUPPETS

**TEMPLATE ON PAGE 63**

- - - - - - - - - - - - - -

**WHAT YOU'LL NEED:** crayons or colored pencils, scissors, tape or glue

- - - - - - - - - - - - - -

**INSTRUCTIONS:**

1 Color all the animals however you like.

2 Cut along the dotted outline.

3 Bend the tabs toward the back of the animals and secure the two ends with tape or glue.

# "READING IS OUT OF THIS WORLD" BOOKMARK

**TEMPLATE ON PAGE 65**

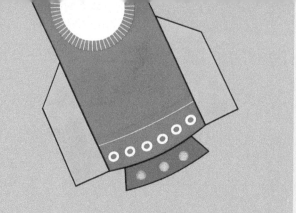

**WHAT YOU'LL NEED:** scissors, hole punch, red yarn, glue

## INSTRUCTIONS:

**1** Cut out the front and back of the rocket bookmark.

**2** Glue the front and back together.

**3** Use a hole punch to make three holes along the bottom of the rocket.

**4** Cut out three strands of red yarn. Make sure they are all the same length.

**5** Fold a strand of yarn in half, and thread the fold through one hole.

**6** Thread the other end of the yarn through the loop and pull it tight to secure it to the rocket.

**7** Do the same with the two remaining yarn strands.

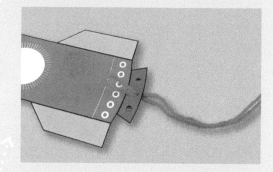

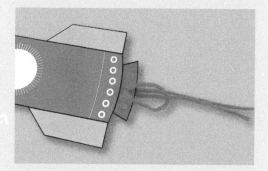

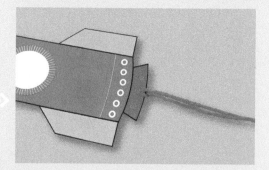

# ACCORDION PENGUIN

**TEMPLATE ON PAGE 67**

- - - - - - - - - - - - - - - - - - - - - -

**WHAT YOU'LL NEED:** scissors, glue

- - - - - - - - - - - - - - - - - - - - - -

**INSTRUCTIONS:**

**1** Cut out the pattern: penguin body, two flippers, and two feet.

**2** Fold the penguin's body like an accordion along the dotted lines, starting at the bottom.

**3** After you are done folding, stretch the folded paper.

**4** Glue the flippers to the penguin's body, one flipper on each side.

**5** Glue the feet at the bottom of the penguin's body.

# DINOSAUR AGAMOGRAPH

**TEMPLATE ON PAGE 69**

- - - - - - - - - - - - - - - - - - -

**WHAT YOU'LL NEED:** scissors

- - - - - - - - - - - - - - - - - - -

**INSTRUCTIONS:**

**1** Cut out the template.

**2** Fold like an accordion. Start with the first rectangle, and fold back and forth from there.

**3** Look at it from one angle to see a dinosaur. Look from the other angle to see a volcano!

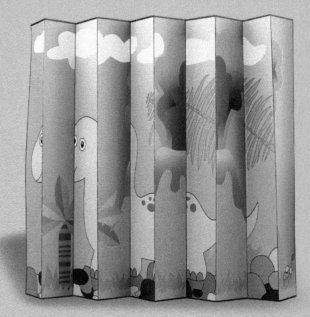

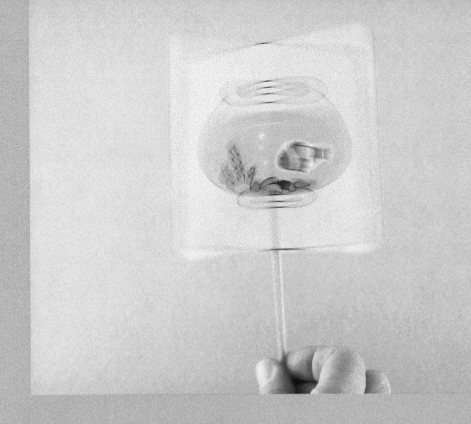

# OPTICAL ILLUSION: FISH IN A BOWL

**TEMPLATE ON PAGE 71**

**WHAT YOU'LL NEED:** scissors, tape, bamboo stick (or straw, or similar), glue

**INSTRUCTIONS:**

1 Cut out the two squares.

2 Tape the bamboo stick to the back of one of the squares.

3 Glue the back of the second square to the back of the first square. The bamboo stick will be wedged between the two squares.

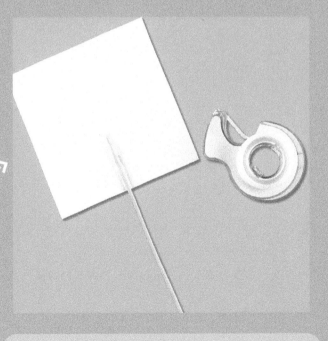

**HOW TO CREATE** the fish-in-the-bowl optical illusion:

1 Spin the bamboo stick between your fingers until you see the fish in the bowl.

# SEASON FORTUNE-TELLER

**TEMPLATE ON PAGE 73**

- - - - - - - - - - - - - - - - - -

**WHAT YOU'LL NEED:** scissors

- - - - - - - - - - - - - - - - - -

## INSTRUCTIONS:

**1** Cut out the fortune-teller pattern. You will have a square.

**2** Fold the paper in half so you can see the snowflake and rain on top, while the leaf and sun are at the bottom.

**3** Open the paper flat and rotate it, then fold it in half the other way. This time the rain and sun will be on top.

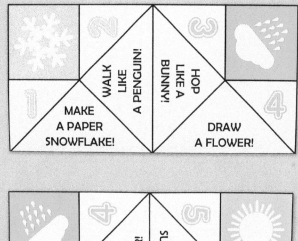

**4** Open the paper flat again, then fold the paper in half diagonally so the top snowflake corner touches the bottom sun corner.

**5** Open the paper flat again, then fold it again along the other diagonal so the top rain corner touches the bottom leaf corner.

**6** Open the paper up and place it facedown.

**7** Fold each corner to the center of the paper. You will now have a smaller square.

**8** Flip the smaller square over, with the images and numbers facedown.

**9** Fold the corners of the smaller square up to the middle of the paper, so that all the numbers face up.

**10** Slide your thumbs and index fingers under the flaps and push the pockets together toward the center of the fortune-teller.

**HOW TO PLAY** with the fortune-teller:

**1** Choose a season on the top of the fortune-teller. Spell it out loud while opening the fortune-teller back and forth, once for each letter. When you get to the last letter of the season, leave the fortune-teller open.

**2** Choose a number from those that are visible and open the fortune-teller back and forth that many times, counting out loud.

**3** Pick another number. Lift the flap with the selected number open to see what seasonal activity you get to do.

# TULIP FLOWER BOUQUET

## TEMPLATE ON PAGE 75

**WHAT YOU'LL NEED:** scissors, glue, three green pipe cleaners

**INSTRUCTIONS:**

**1** Cut out the nine flower pieces.

**2** Fold all the pieces in half lengthwise.

**3** Group the pieces by color. You will have three red pieces, three pink pieces, and three purple pieces.

**4** Put together the red tulip first. Apply glue on the back half of the first red piece. Stick the first piece to the back half of the second piece, lining up the edges. Glue the third piece to the second piece in the same way. Before you glue the third piece to the first piece, slide a green pipe cleaner between the pieces.

**5** Repeat the previous step for the pink and purple flowers.

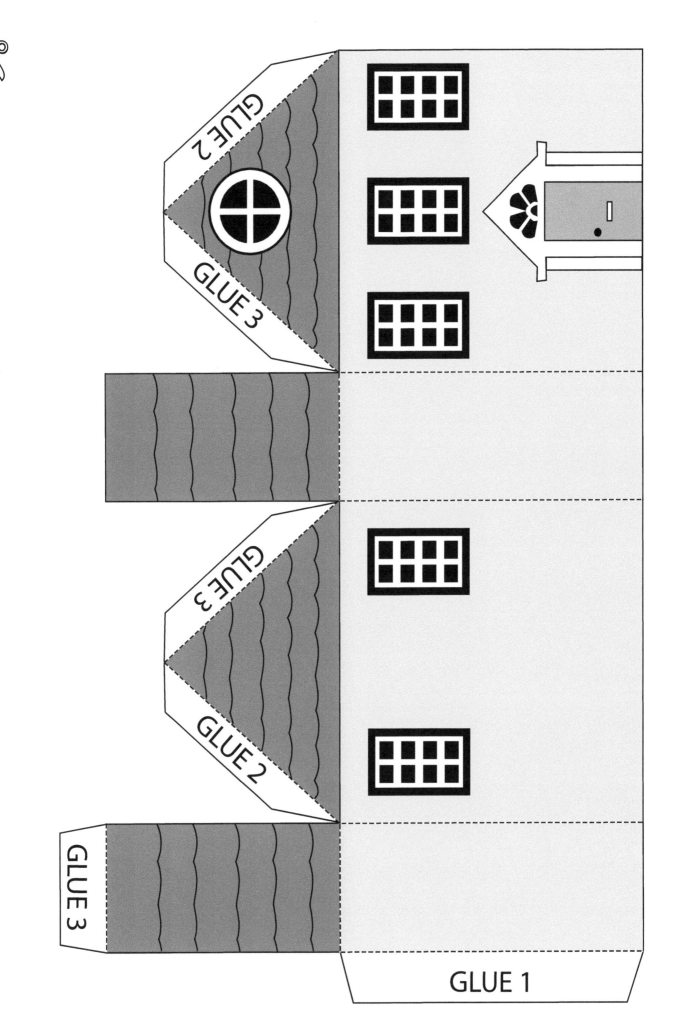

GLUE 2

GLUE 3

GLUE 3

GLUE 2

GLUE 3

GLUE 1

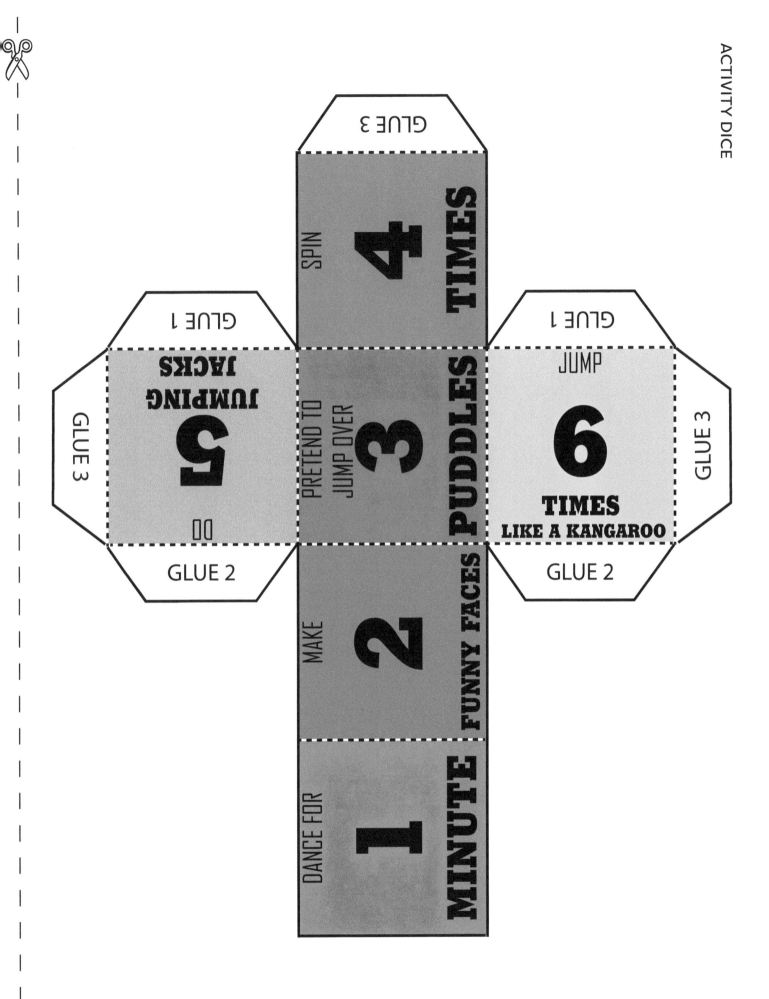

GLUE 3

SPIN **4** TIMES

GLUE 1

JUMPING JACKS **5** DO

PRETEND TO JUMP OVER **3** PUDDLES

JUMP **6** TIMES LIKE A KANGAROO

GLUE 1

GLUE 3

GLUE 2

GLUE 2

MAKE **2** FUNNY FACES

DANCE FOR **1** MINUTE

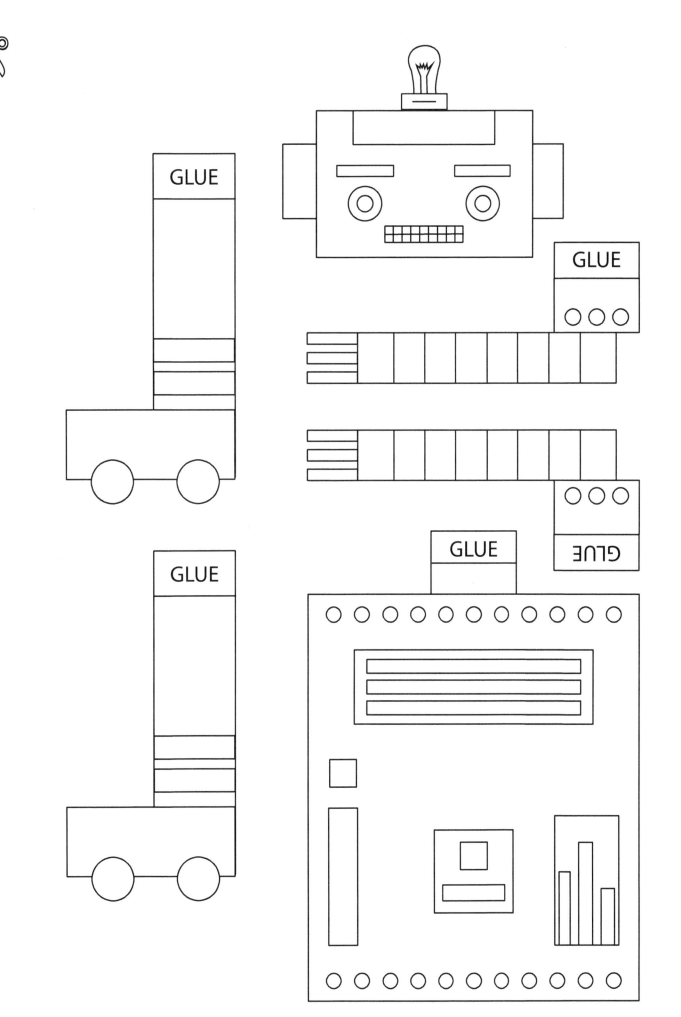

GLUE

GLUE

GLUE

GLUE

GLUE

TO:

..............................................

FROM:

..............................................

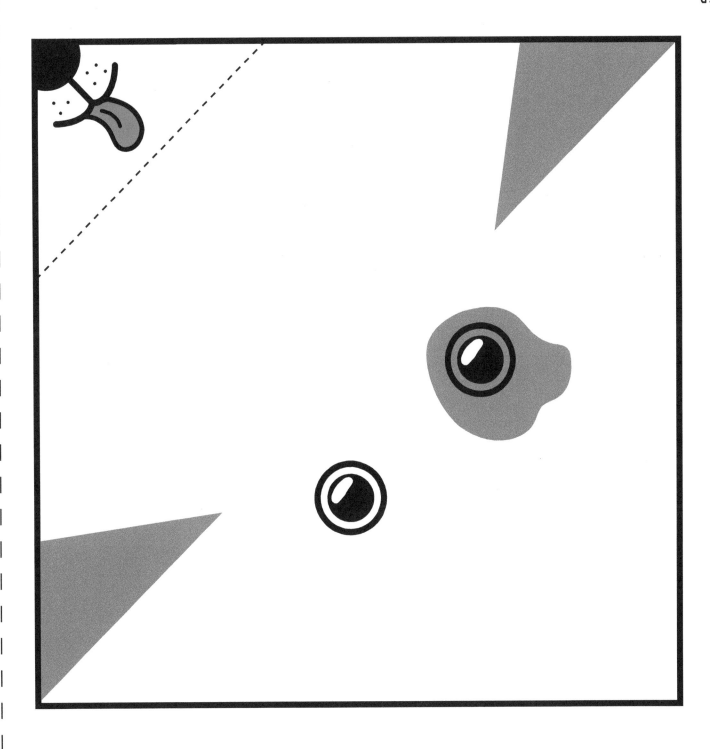

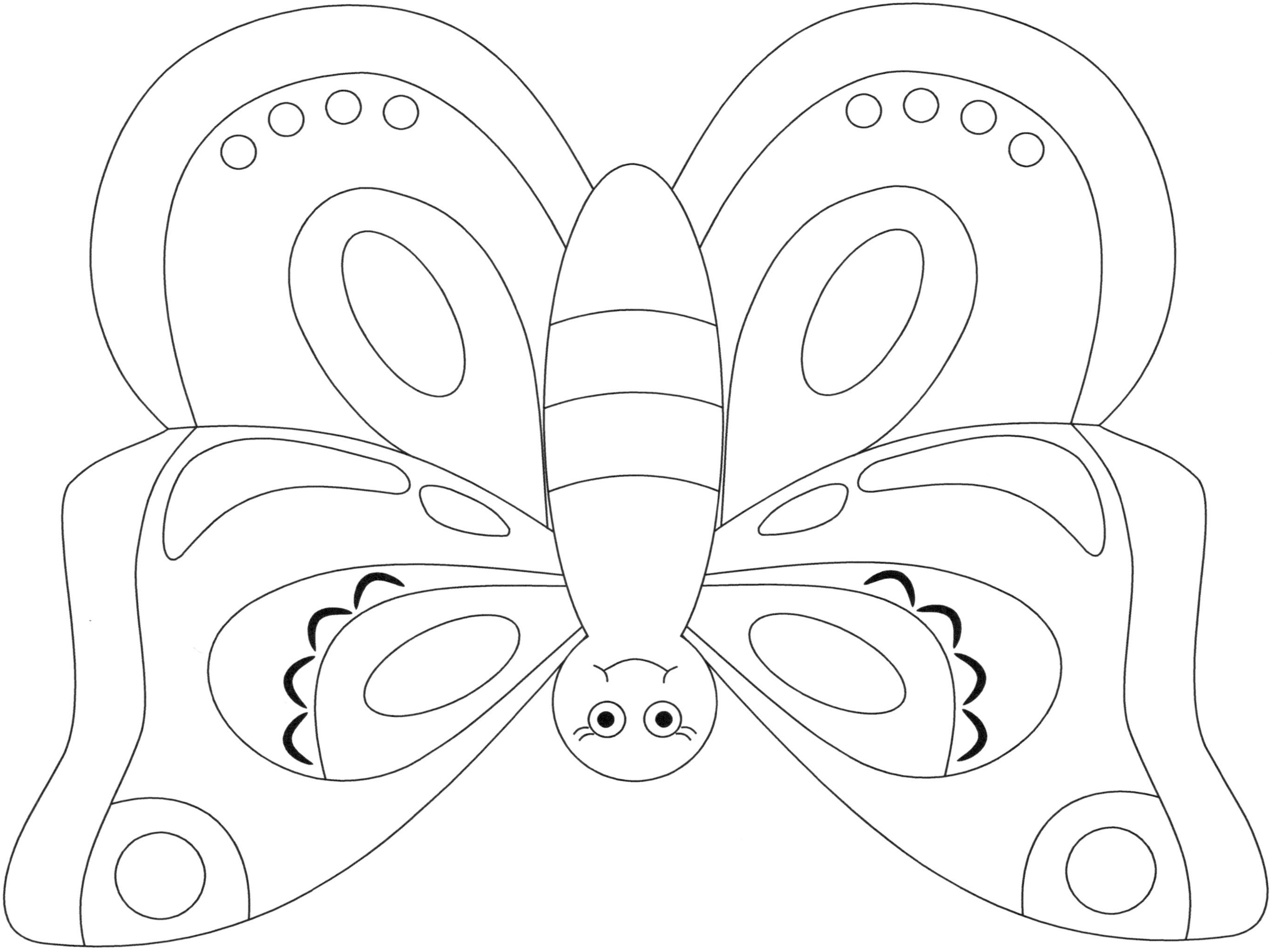

LINE 1

LINE 2

Reading
is out of
this world!

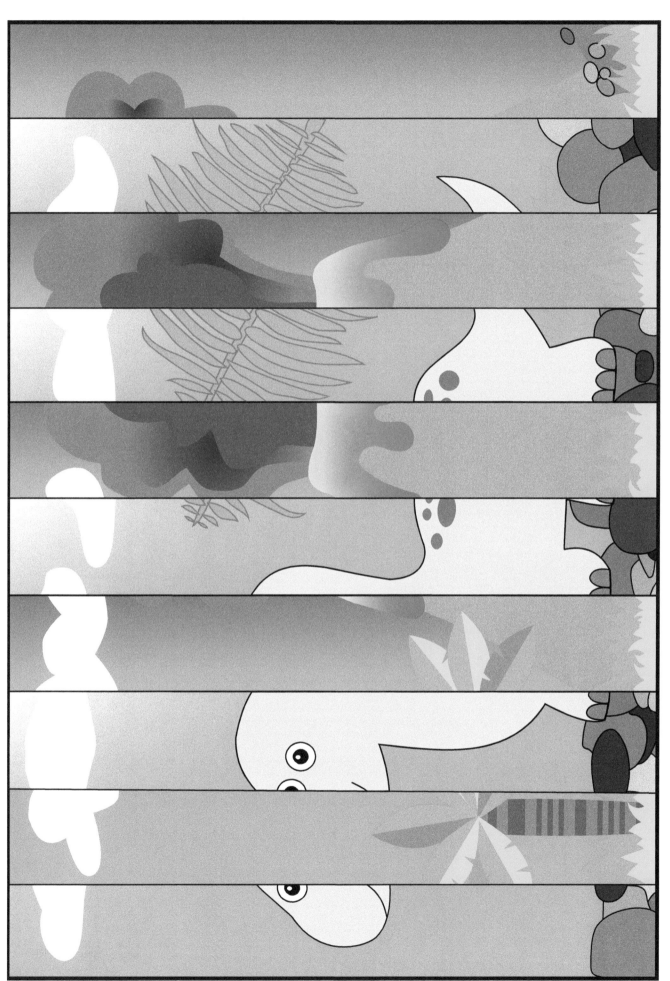

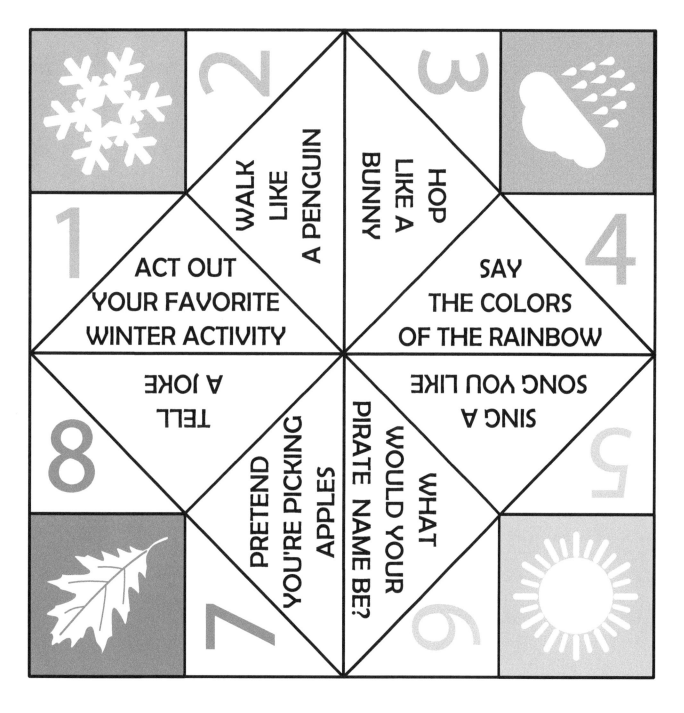

CPSIA information can be obtained
at www.ICGtesting.com
Printed in the USA
BVHW09204520522
637632BV00006B/14